—A TRAVELER'S GUIDE TO—

DEATH VALLEY NATIONAL PARK

— CLIFF LAWSON —

© 2003 Death Valley Natural History Association

Second Printing, with changes

Author: Cliff Lawson
Copyeditor: Sue Irwin
Graphic Designer: Sue Irwin
Photo Editor: John Evarts
Maps: Sue Irwin
Death Valley NHA Coordinator: Esy Fields
Printed on recycled paper by
Paragon Press, Salt Lake City, Utah

Produced for Death Valley Natural History Association by
Cachuma Press
Post Office Box 560
Los Olivos, California 93441

To order this book, please contact the publisher at:
Death Valley Natural History Association
P.O. Box 188
Death Valley, California 92328
(760) 786-2146

Library of Congress Catalog Card Number: 96-84824
ISBN: 1-878-900-30-7

Front Cover: Zabriskie Point vista. LARRY ULRICH
Back Cover: Saline Valley. ANDY SELTERS
Title Page Spread: Death Valley Dunes. TOM TILL
Opposite: Cracked mud at dunes' edge. GEORGE WARD

ABOUT THE AUTHOR

Cliff Lawson moved to Death Valley in 1989, when his wife accepted a position as a Park Service archaeologist. During the next three years he hiked the Valley extensively, winter and summer, while researching a book on desert survival.

Cliff holds a B.A. in Anthropology from the University of Massachusetts and a J.D. from Harvard Law School. He lives in Ridgecrest, California, where he works for the Navy's Technical Information Division at China Lake. He also does freelance writing.

CONTENTS

INTRODUCTION

In the past century, dozens of writers have chronicled Death Valley. I suspect that all of them faced the same problem I did. The toughest task in writing about this unique corner of the earth is not finding what to put in. It's deciding what to leave out. Far more exists between the Panamint Range and the Amargosa Range than can fit between the covers of a single book. And Death Valley National Park now extends well beyond Death Valley, encompassing Saline Valley, Eureka Valley, and a large part of Panamint Valley as well.

This guide therefore is an overview; a sampling of the Park's highlights. The text, maps, and photos in these pages will show you what you can experience in Death Valley if you have a day or two, or three. A week, if you're lucky.

Each of the guide's six chapters covers a different section of the Park. Chapters are

further divided into individual destination write-ups. Before heading out, read about your intended destinations to see if you'll want to bring along anything special (a picnic lunch, topographic maps, extra film, hiking gear, etc.). Figure to spend a *minimum* of one day exploring each chapter's destinations.

Whether this is your first visit to Death Valley or your fiftieth, you are part of a grand tradition. For more than 10,000 years, people have been coming to Death Valley. First were the hunters with spears and atlatls, stalking bighorn sheep near the Valley's springs. Then the climate grew dry and hot, hotter even than it is now, and people seldom entered the Valley. Some 5,000 years ago, the climate became wet again and the hunters returned. A lake formed on the Valley floor (30 feet deep—a mere shadow of the 600-foot-deep lake that had filled the Valley in the Pleistocene, but the climatic cycle continued and the shallow lake dried up.

About 2,000 years ago other hunters arrived, this time carrying bows and arrows. Despite the technological edge over their predecessors, the new arrivals found tough times. Game was smaller, and seeds and roots became a part of the diet. Finally, about 1,000 years ago, a group of people entered the Valley bearing a distinctly new type of arrowhead as well as the skills to make pottery. They crafted pits in which to

Above: Desert cloudbursts scour the hills, sending muddy water into the washes. GEORGE WARD
Left: Native American rock art in Death Valley often depicts bighorn sheep. RANDI HIRSCHMANN

store mesquite beans and used metates and manos to grind and process seeds. These people were the Desert Shoshone, and they have been here ever since.

In the Valley and on adjacent slopes, the people hunted sheep, deer, rabbits, and lizards. As the seasons changed, the Shoshone moved about the Death Valley region, harvesting plants and seeds. The arrival in 1849 of emigrants from the east, followed soon by an influx of miners who took control of the water sources, had a major destabilizing effect on Shoshone lifestyle. Hostilities between the Shoshone and the newcomers flared, but were settled with the Treaty of Ruby Valley in 1866.

Through the years that followed the Shoshone adapted to the changed environment, working as guides, miners, wood choppers, domestic helpers, and ranch hands. Later, they participated in the construction of Scotty's Castle and Furnace Creek Inn. The interest of both the Tribe and the National Park are enhanced by recognition of their coexistence on the same land and by establishing partnerships for compatible land uses and for the interpretation of the Tribe's history and culture for visitors to the Park.

Gold had drawn white settlers to Death Valley in the mid-nineteenth century. Discovery of silver, lead, borax, and a host of lesser-known minerals made mining the principal activity in Death Valley until the 1920s. But as the traveling public traded horseshoes for rubber tires, and America began to hear of the incredible sights and experiences the Valley offered, tourism surged. In 1933 Death Valley was proclaimed a National Monument by President Hoover. The California Desert Protection Act, signed by President Clinton in 1994, created Death Valley National Park, more than half again larger than the National Monument.

Major attractions for Death Valley visitors are its rugged natural beauty and some of the most spectacular scenery in the national park system. However, nature also shows a harsh edge here. Along with the fabled extremes of heat and aridity, high winds (up to 80 miles per hour) sometimes whip the Valley. Flash floods can fill a bone-dry ravine with a raging torrent in minutes. Rattlesnakes, black widow spiders, and cactus spines await the unwary.

People have added their own threats. Abandoned mine shafts and tunnels are potential death traps. Backcountry roads serve up jagged rocks that can gut an oil pan or snap an axle. Many of the Valley's major roads are narrow and winding; speeding and inattentive drivers cause many accidents each year. All of these dangers are compounded by long distances to medical or mechanical assistance.

Unexpected pleasures also await the Death Valley visitor. Try waiting in the predawn cool of morning at Dante's View for that perfect moment to click the camera shutter and record one of the world's grandest views. Roll headlong down the face of a sand dune, then struggle back up to the top and do it again. Immerse your road-tired body in a breathtaking hot spring, 60 miles from the nearest telephone.

People can, and do, drive through Death Valley without ever getting out of the car. But if you are willing to meet Death Valley on its own terms—rugged country, long distances, nature at its most spectacular and least inhibited—your visit here will be one of the most rewarding experiences of your life.

TRAVEL AND SAFETY TIPS

The guide assumes you are traveling in a two-wheel-drive vehicle, but aren't afraid to drive a few miles on a dirt road. It also presupposes that you are not a specialist in desert survival, but that you have the common sense to follow a few basic principles for your own protection and the Park's:

- *Always carry extra water.* A full plastic gallon jug for each person in your party is a minimum.
- *Always check road conditions.* In any season, the road that was passable yesterday may be washed out tomorrow. Conditions are posted at Furnace Creek and Stovepipe Wells, or ask a ranger.
- *Always let someone know where you are going and when you'll be back.* If you don't show up on time, help can be sent.
- *Never drive off road.* This includes bicycles. The delicate ecosystems can't handle vehicle traffic, and the fines for violating this rule are stiff.
- *Ask for help when you need it.* Park Service personnel, California Highway Patrol officers, and County Sheriff's deputies all want you to have a happy and safe trip. They will be glad to provide you with advice and assistance.
- *Remove nothing from the Park that you didn't bring with you or buy here.* Not so much as a shiny pebble, a dried flower, or a rusted nail. Regulations protecting the Park's natural and cultural resources are strictly enforced.

1

FURNACE CREEK AREA

Furnace Creek is an excellent place to start your tour of Death Valley. Within a short distance (short by Death Valley standards), you will discover spectacular scenery, geologic wonders and curiosities, and historic artifacts that bring Death Valley's distant past to life. You also have the opportunity to taste the subtler attractions of the Valley: the vastness of 80-mile views and a quietness so intense that it rings in the ears. After a day spent visiting the destinations described in this chapter, you will begin to understand the allure of Death Valley, and why more than a million people visit here each year.

FURNACE CREEK

104 miles from Lone Pine via Highways 136 and 190. 123 miles from Ridgecrest via Highways 178 and 190. 57 miles from Shoshone via Highways 127 and 190 (or 69 miles via Highway 178/Badwater Road and Highway 190). 41 miles from Beatty via Highway 374, Beatty Cutoff Road and Highway 190. Map on page 2.

Furnace Creek is the heart of Death Valley National Park. Not the geographic center—that would be a point somewhere near the head of Tucki Wash—but the administrative, cultural, recreational, and economic core. This 4-square-mile cluster of buildings and facilities near the mouth of Furnace Creek Wash sets the rhythm of life for visitors to the nation's largest and most varied desert park.

Here the National Park Service operates the Park Headquarters, overseeing an area that's larger than the state of Connecticut. Next door is a decades-old date grove originally planted in the 1930s as a cash crop; today it adds to the oasis feel of the area. In a nearby 314-acre village are the homes of about 50 Timbisha Shoshone, descendants of Death Valley's earliest inhabitants. Just up the road, visitors from around the world enjoy the elegance of champagne brunches at Furnace Creek Inn.

Furnace Creek also offers the Park's largest collection of services: accommodations (from tent sites to luxurious suites), restaurants (coffee shop to fine dining), stores (groceries, gifts, essentials), sports (swimming, horseback riding, golf), an airstrip, a full-service gas station, and two museums. And of course, the Death Valley Post Office, Zip Code 92328. The Furnace Creek Inn and Ranch are privately owned inholdings within the Park.

Opposite: Zabriskie Point offers a grand vista of Death Valley and the Panamints. LARRY ULRICH
Below: The Park Service Visitor Center houses the Death Valley Museum. MARK J. DOLYAK

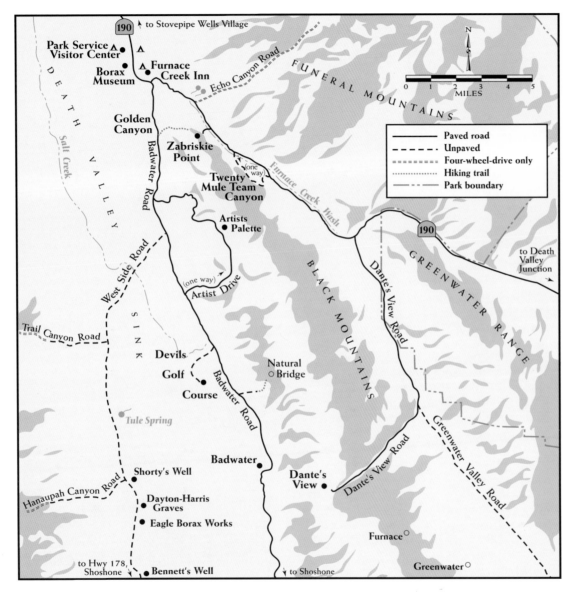

Although Furnace Creek holds the western hemisphere's all-time high temperature record (134° F on July 10, 1913), the name does not allude to that record, nor to the smothering heat a visitor will experience here in the summer. It refers to an actual furnace, built near the canyon mouth by Asabel Bennett in 1860 to test ore samples for silver. Long gone, of course, is that small stone furnace. Nor does the creek run here any longer. Its water, which came from nearby Travertine Springs, is now piped throughout the Furnace Creek complex for domestic, commercial, and irrigation purposes.

PARK SERVICE VISITOR CENTER

Located on Highway 190 at the center of the Furnace Creek complex. Map on this page.

A low brown building on the west side of Highway 190 houses both the Visitor Center and Death Valley National Park Headquarters. Parking is on the south side. As soon as you enter the building—and before you get sidetracked with the wealth of information the Visitor Center has to offer—pay the Park entrance fee at the lobby counter. Save the receipt until you leave the Park.

In the auditorium, to the left of the entrance, slide orientation programs are presented each half hour. Ranger talks and evening programs are also presented in the auditorium—check the schedule.

About one-third of the Visitor Center is taken up by the museum. You can breeze through the museum in five minutes or spend a solid hour or more studying the exhibits and learning about the history, biology, botany, geology, and meteorology of Death Valley.

A fascinating exhibit is the 10-foot by 20-foot relief map of Death Valley, built for the Park Service in 1986 by a Missouri artist. Spend a few minutes here tracing out your day's itinerary. This will give you a good feel for the driving distances ahead and a sense of where your destinations are in the overall context of the Park.

At the Visitor Center's bookstore, you'll find over 700 titles (in several languages) covering the Mojave Desert, and Death Valley in particular. Death Valley videotapes and children's books are also available.

An excellent investment is the weatherproof map of Death Valley, which contains a level of detail sufficient for all but the most hard-core backcountry hiker, and information on safety and Park regulations. If you need more detailed maps, the book shop also stocks U.S. Geologic Survey 7.5-minute topographic maps for the Valley.

The most valuable information resources at the Visitor Center stand behind the counter at the lobby and wear the uniform of the National Park Service. The rangers who staff the information counter know this Park inside out and can answer any question you'll have about Death Valley. They also have dozens of handouts covering everything from how Death Valley got its name to identifying local animals.

Before you leave the Visitor Center, you'll want to check the daily updated weather and road conditions. Rainstorms, sometimes violent and always unpredictable, can render the Valley's main roads impassable.

Left: Park rangers staff the Visitor Center.
FRED HIRSCHMANN
Right: A locomotive at the Borax Museum once hauled Death Valley's borate ore. MARK J. DOLYAK

BORAX MUSEUM

Drive 0.3 mile south of the Visitor Center on Highway 190 to the Furnace Creek Ranch complex on your right, and park inside the entrance. You can also walk from the Visitor Center, pausing to rest at the shaded picnic tables in front of the Death Valley date farm. Map on page 2.

As you walk through the doors of the Borax Museum, you're entering the oldest wood-frame structure in Death Valley. It was built around 1883 by the legendary Francis Marion "Borax" Smith as the assay office at Monte Blanco. (You can see its original setting in your drive through Twenty Mule Team Canyon.) The building was moved to Furnace Creek in the 1950s.

The museum contains an amazing collection that chronicles the history of Death Valley. Artifacts range in size from an exquisite fingernail-sized Shoshone obsidian arrow point to a 60-ton oil-burning locomotive that once hauled borate ore from Ryan to Death Valley

Junction. Among the museum highlights are an exceptional collection of minerals, fine examples of Shoshone basketry, and a beautiful Shoshone bandolier made of flicker feathers.

On the museum's 3/4-acre back lot are more than 60 displays illustrating the simple but effective tools and technologies of early Death Valley mining and transportation. The inexpensive *Self-Guided Tour Book*, available at the museum desk, has a note on the history and use of every item here. Admission to Borax Museum is free.

FURNACE CREEK INN

1 mile south of the Visitor Center on Highway 190. As the highway makes a gentle uphill curve to the east, you see Furnace Creek Inn on your left. Map on page 2.

Construction of the Furnace Creek Inn marked the transition of Death Valley from a mining economy to a tourist attraction. Huge borate deposits discovered in 1926 near Boron, California, sounded the death knell for the Valley's multimillion-dollar borate industry.

Frank Jenifer, manager of the Tonopah and Tidewater Railroad, saw the writing on the wall. He convinced Pacific

Top: An 1880s arrastra is displayed outside the Borax Museum. ROLAND AND KAREN MUSCHENETZ
Bottom: Fine stonework is featured at Furnace Creek Inn, opened in 1927. FRANK S. BALTHIS
Opposite: Uplifted mudstones from an ancient lake have been sculpted into today's badlands near Zabriskie Point. PAT O'HARA

Coast Borax Company to build a hotel at the mouth of Furnace Creek Wash, a site that offered a stunning panoramic view of the Valley and ample water from Travertine Springs, a mile up the wash. Noted Los Angeles architect Albert Martin was called in to design the building, and in the fall of 1926, Paiute and Shoshone laborers began making adobe bricks for the project. Construction began the day after Thanksgiving. Steve Esteves, a stonemason from Madrid, created the inn's elegant stonework and graceful retaining walls using local fieldstone. The doors opened in February 1927.

Today Furnace Creek Inn hosts visitors from around the world. It vies only with Scotty's Castle (see Chapter 4) for the honor of being the most magnificent building in Death Valley.

ZABRISKIE POINT

4.5 miles south of the Visitor Center via Highway 190. As you pass Furnace Creek Inn, you enter Furnace Creek Wash, which drains the canyon that divides the Amargosa Range into the Funeral Mountains and the Black Mountains. You pass the entrance to Echo Canyon on your left (high-clearance vehicles only) before reaching the Zabriskie Point turnoff on your right. Map on page 2.

Here is one of the loveliest views in Death Valley, and one of the most accessible. In fact the hardest part about getting here is the 200-yard climb from the parking lot to the viewing area—but there are several benches where you can stop and take a breather. This site is named for Christian Breevort Zabriskie, a 36-year veteran of the Pacific Coast Borax Company.

From the point, you look out over a maze of rippling yellow mudstone hills that were part of a lake bed several million years ago. Dark lava caps on some of the hills to the south and east have resisted erosion more than the chaotic, wrinkled hills around you, known as the badlands. Above the badlands, to the west, you can see a bit of the floor of Death Valley. Beyond that, from the mouth of Blackwater Wash in the Panamint Range, sprawls a huge alluvial fan, a semicircular deposit containing millions of tons of rock washed onto the Valley floor by the erosional forces of rainstorms and snowmelt.

To your right as you look out over the Valley is a sharp hill shaped like a shark's tooth (particularly impressive when awash in the golden light of sunrise). This is Manly Beacon, named for William Lewis Manly. In 1849, a group of gold seekers were stranded for a month in Death Valley at Bennett's Well (see Chapter 2) until Manly and another man hiked out through the Panamints, found a route to civilization (present-day Saugus), and returned with supplies. As the rescued party left Death Valley, one member is purported to have looked back from the crest of the Pana-mints and uttered the famous phrase from whence the Valley takes its name:

"Good-bye, Death Valley."

An easy, pleasant hike of about 2.7 miles begins at Zabriskie Point and winds past the foot of Manly Beacon and down Golden Canyon. This hike is fun almost any time in moderate weather (bring plenty of water), but be extremely cautious during high summer temperatures. The hike is spellbinding when taken at night during a full moon. The trail starts from the west side of the Zabriskie Point parking area. You can also hike this in the other direction, from Golden Canyon (see Chapter 2).

TWENTY MULE TEAM CANYON

5.5 miles south of the Visitor Center via Highway 190. Map on page 2.

Whether or not this narrow, twisting, 2.8-mile road ever felt the hooves of 20-mule teams is a matter of conjecture. But that it was the site of extensive borax workings is obvious from the many prospect holes scattered at various elevations along the sides of the canyon. These tunnels are not safe to explore, but with a strong flashlight they are interesting to look into. Note the odd flashes of light thrown from gypsum and occasional colemanite crystals.

The road, which runs one way from west to east, is dusty most of the year. Climbing generally upward, it passes through terrain similar to the badlands below Zabriskie Point: low yellow-brown hills, eroded and barren of vegetation save for a scattering of desert holly bushes.

At about 1.8 miles the road begins to bear left, leaving the main canyon. Close to this point sat the old Monte Blanco assay office, the building that now houses the Borax Museum at Furnace Creek. The large dark hill to the right is Monte Blanco (White Hill), three million tons of rich borate ore that shows as white streaks on the brown hillside. Continuing north, you top a rise and suddenly head down a steep hill. From the bottom of that hill, it's 0.8 mile back to Highway 190.

DANTE'S VIEW

25 miles from the Visitor Center. Take Highway 190 south 12.5 miles to Dante's View Road (paved), turn right, and continue another 12.5 miles to Dante's View. (Trailers must park 5 miles before the lookout.) A mile south of 190 on Dante's View Road you pass the Billie Mine, a borate mine owned by U.S. Borax and Chemical Company. On the hillside beyond is Ryan, a mining town built for borax workers in the 1920s. The Billie Mine and Ryan are private property and not open to the public. About 7.5 miles from Highway 190 you pass Greenwater Valley Road, which heads south to the old boomtown sites of Greenwater and Furnace. Map on page 2.

If a person were to be allowed only one brief glance into the heart of Death Valley, just a single sweep of the eyes with which to record its visual splendor, there could be no other place to take that opportunity than at Dante's View.

In April of 1926, several far-sighted

businessmen—railroad and borax people aware of the potential for tourism—were searching for a location with the grandest view of Death Valley. They had almost settled on Chloride Cliff in the Funeral Mountains when Deputy Sheriff Charlie Brown of Greenwater brought them to this remote peak in the Black Mountains. The group was instantly converted and promptly named the spot Dante's View.

From this vantage point a mile above sea level, you look west straight out across the Valley to Telescope Peak, the highest point in the Panamint Range. At 11,049 feet, Telescope is yet a mile higher than Dante's View. Spilling out from the canyons of the Panamints are broad interlocking alluvial fans.

Beyond Telescope Peak in the far distance is the crest of the Sierra Nevada near 14,495-foot Mount Whitney, the highest point in the lower 48 states. Shift your gaze downward to the Valley floor and you see Badwater (282 feet below sea level), the lowest point on this continent.

Extremes of altitude aside, the view is incredible: fixed in its geologic magnificence, yet changing constantly in color and shading with weather conditions and the time of day. A particularly good time

to visit is early morning.

On the floor of Death Valley, the most striking feature is the white expanse of dried salt crystals that form the salt pans. Sometimes after heavy rains the lowest areas are filled with shallow lakes that reflect the mountains and sky.

To the east the Amargosa Desert rolls away from the Black Mountains and out into Nevada. The view encompasses several Great Basin ranges, culminating in the Spring Mountains (with Charleston

Peak at 11,918 feet) just west of Las Vegas.

For an even more spectacular view— and a good workout at this altitude— follow the rocky 350-yard path along a ridge line that starts at the parking area and extends out into the Valley. For the more adventurous, a longer trail runs north along the mountain crest from the parking area. Back down the road at the bottom of the hill, below the lookout area and out of the wind, are restrooms and picnic tables.

2

SOUTHERN DEATH VALLEY

This chapter takes you on a great loop through the southern half of Death Valley. Following Badwater Road and West Side Road, you'll drive, walk, and clamber through fasci-nating geological phenomena and see evidence of mining history spanning more than a century.

One day is too little time to experience everything discussed here. Some

Opposite: In wet years, Salt Creek flows into Death Valley's salt pans. JIM STIMSON
Below: Outcrops in Golden Canyon. MARK J. DOLYAK

areas demand four-wheel-drive, high-clearance vehicles with stout-hearted drivers. Take time to choose where you'll visit, based on your interests, the time available, and your vehicle. Discuss road conditions with the Visitor Center staff or with any ranger you meet. And before you start, top off your water jugs.

GOLDEN CANYON

3 miles south of the Visitor Center via Highway 190 and Badwater Road. If approaching from the north, be careful of oncoming traffic as you pull into the parking area. Map on page 2.

Built in the late 1920s during Death Valley's first flush of tourist enthusiasm, a narrow paved strip of a road once wound through Golden Canyon. Along this road, occasional Packards or Model A's chugged the twisting 1.5 miles to Red Cathedral. Today, odd pieces of pavement still lie askew in the narrows, left here when a flash flood ripped

away the road more than 25 years ago. Now Golden Canyon offers one of the prettiest and easiest canyon hikes in Death Valley.

A helpful interpretive guide is available at the parking area. Keyed to numbered signs along the trail, this pamphlet explains the geology of the canyon.

Golden Canyon is best seen in the late afternoon, when the light brings out the rich golden color of the canyon walls. As you travel through the Park you will find that most geologic features show—and photograph—best in early morning or late afternoon light. The atmospherically filtered sunlight enlivens the colors, particularly the red shades, and the low angle of the sun's rays throws even the smallest surface features into sharp relief.

The most impressive vistas are at the head of the canyon, about 1.5 miles from the parking area, where the 400-foot-high

is the spot to take your pictures; the best light is from mid–afternoon on.

A geologist will look at these colors and see hematite, limonite, and chemically altered deposits of volcanic ash and cinder dating from 6 to 14 million years ago—part of the 4,000-foot-thick Artist Drive Formation. Still, understanding the cause of the colors does not lessen their magic.

Artist Drive is a wonderful ride for youngsters, not only for the color but also for the swooping dips and turns. The road uncoils like a sidewinder as it weaves through the chaotic geology of the hills, giving extraordinary close-ups of depositional and erosional features. See if you can spot a miniature Manly Beacon on the left 7.7 miles into the drive.

wall of the Red Cathedral reigns dark and massive next to the sheer yellow flank of Manly Beacon. The iron–oxide–stained "cathedral" is part of an ancient alluvial fan long since cemented into a hard, erosion–resistant fanglomerate. Its redness stands in bright contrast to the golden mudstone hills and the deep blue Death Valley sky.

About a mile into the canyon is the cutoff for the trail to Zabriskie Point (Chapter 1). Winding another 1.7 miles through these badlands, typical of the geology of the northern end of the Black Mountains, the trail provides an in–your–face view of Manly Beacon and ends at the parking area below Zabriskie Point.

ARTIST DRIVE

9.5 miles south of the Visitor Center via Highway 190 and Badwater Road. The 9-mile-long Artist Drive loop runs one way south to north, commencing and ending at Badwater Road. Map on page 2.

From the highway, there is no clue as to what lies along this paved road stretching toward the Black Mountains. Half a mile in you begin to see the colors in the rocks ahead, smears of red, pink, orange, and green in finely graded shades that only artists have names for.

Artists Palette, about 4.5 miles into the drive, is "painted" with a profusion of colors that somehow work together. Here

DEVIL'S GOLF COURSE

13 miles south of the Visitor Center via Highway 190 and Badwater Road. A parking area and interpretive sign are located at the end of a bumpy, 1.3-mile gravel road heading west from the highway. Devil's Golf Course is also crossed by the north end of West Side Road about 2 miles from Badwater Road. Map on page 2.

Describing this expanse of bizarrely textured salt pan, the Park Service's first Death Valley guidebook, published in 1934, noted, "only the devil could play golf on such a surface." It is hard to conceive of playing anything on these tortured convolutions.

The ground is nearly pure sodium

chloride (table salt), stained brown by silt and mud. Pressure exerted by growing salt crystals thrusts the ground upward in erratic shapes, and the landscape is further shaped by the erosional forces of wind and water. In every direction are spikes, pits, mushrooms, craters, and jumbled, jagged ridges in dizzying density. As the 1934 guide noted, "a flat space large enough to lay one's hat cannot be found."

Near the parking area, where many feet have ventured out onto the salt, the worn surface has a rounded, almost benign appearance. Walk out farther to get

a truer feel, but step carefully, since the footing is treacherous and this is nasty stuff to fall on. A five-minute walk will take you far enough to get a sense of the utter desolation that an early traveler might have felt here.

Devil's Golf Course parallels Badwater Road for about 10 miles. The area is part of 200 square miles of salt pan or salt flats that reach from Salt Creek in the north to Shoreline Butte in the south. The flats are the remains of a shallow lake that evaporated about two thousand years ago.

Calcite and other carbonates first precipitated from the shrinking lake. As the lake continued to give up moisture to the desiccating air at a faster rate than the water could be replenished, sulfates such as gypsum began to precipitate. Finally the dying lake gave up its chlorides before disappearing in the geologic blink of an eye. Chlorides comprise much of the Valley floor. Beneath Devil's Golf Course the sandwiched layers of chlorides and other sediments are about 1,000 feet thick.

Opposite: Hikers explore the colorful terrain near Artists Palette. JIM STROUP
Left: Sodium chloride (table salt) covers much of the Death Valley floor. RANDI HIRSCHMANN
Right: Crystal growth and erosion create a tortured surface at Devil's Golf Course. ERIC WUNROW

BADWATER

18 miles south of the Visitor Center via Highway 190 and Badwater Road. (The turnoff to Natural Bridge is 3 miles north of Badwater. Access to this massive arch of stone is by a rough 1.6-mile dirt road followed by an easy quarter-mile hike.) Map on page 2.

In naming Badwater, an early Death Valley surveyor relied on his burro's discriminating taste. Viewing the shallow pool of water here, which rests atop a bed of salt-rich sediments, one is not tempted to corroborate the burro's finding. In an age when water comes from taps and bottles, it is difficult to conceive of how precious an open, easily accessible source of water once was in Death Valley. And how terrible the disappointment when that water proved unpalatable.

The remarkable feature that distinguishes Badwater from any other spot in the western hemisphere is its elevation. Or rather, its lack of elevation. At 279-and-a-fraction feet below sea level, Badwater is about as close as most people will get to the center of the earth. For the purist, there are a couple of spots that are 3 feet lower. These unmarked sites are 4 miles west of Badwater.

To best appreciate where you are in relationship to the world's baseline for elevation measurements, turn around and look up at the wall of the Black Mountains. More than 250 feet above you on the nearly vertical rock face is a plain white sign with just two words: Sea Level. Death Valley is the lowest point in the Western Hemisphere and the fifth lowest

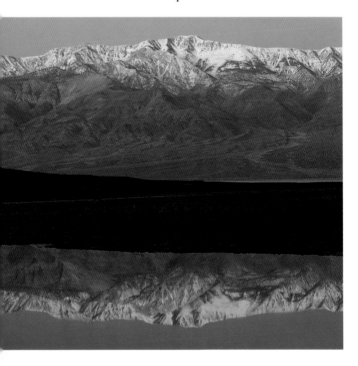

point in the world.

Like Devil's Golf Course, Badwater is a spot where a little walking can convey the sense of desolation that must have overwhelmed the Manly party nearly a century and a half ago. Grab a water bottle and strike westward for a short walk. Follow the trail across the salt flats, out away from the highway and the parked cars, into the interminable expanse of the Valley floor. Then stop and imagine being out here with no roads, no maps, little food or water, the sun beating down from above, the harsh salt beneath your feet, and only the dream of gold somewhere beyond the Panamints to sustain you. You can turn and walk back to your car. They could only press on.

If you continue south from Badwater, in 23 miles you'll reach the south end of West Side Road (see next entry) and just beyond that, Shoreline Butte. Clearly visible across the face of this 650-foot-high basalt hill are shorelines cut by the wind-driven waves of Lake Manly. The lake once extended 90 miles through Death Valley and, at its height, reached within 50 feet of the Butte's peak.

Past Shoreline Butte another 1.3 miles is Ashford Mill. Here, 80 years ago, a 40-ton roller mill processed gold ore from a mine 5 miles to the east. (A hike to the mine makes a good day trip.) One building still stands at the mill. From inside, you can take scenic photos of Shoreline Butte and the Owlshead Mountains framed in the building's crumbling door

and window frames.

Below Ashford Mill, Badwater Road swings east at Ashford Junction. Beyond this point, it is another 24 miles through 3,288-foot Salsberry Pass to the town of Shoshone.

A four-wheel-drive road running south just below Ashford Junction heads 24 miles to Saratoga Spring, where three large ponds comprise a sanctuary for birds and waterfowl. This was once a wagon stop on the 20-mule-team route between the Amargosa Borax Works and Dagget, and it was here in 1886 that teamster Al Bryson was killed with a shovel by his helper Sterling Wassam after an argument over a dull can opener. This oasis is home to one of the four species of pupfish found in Death Valley region.

WEST SIDE ROAD

The north end of West Side Road begins 7 miles south of the Visitor Center via Highway 190 and Badwater Road. Conditions along this 45-mile-long gravel road vary, but generally you'll average about 25 miles per hour. Map on page 2.

For the first few miles, West Side Road cuts directly southwest across the Valley floor, leaving the Black Mountains behind and heading straight for Telescope Peak, the highest peak in the Panamint Range. Two miles from the highway you enter Devil's Golf Course and cross Salt Creek, which flows south toward Badwater. As you drive out of the salt flats, the first sign of plant life you see are pickleweed and salt grass,

Above: The ruins of Ashford Mill date back to a 1915 gold-mining operation. GEORGE WUERTHNER *Opposite: At Badwater, elevation 279 feet below sea level, shallow pools reflect the snow-covered summit of Telescope Peak at elevation 11,049.* PAT O'HARA

which thrive in the saline soil.

Soon the road swings to the south past the Trail Canyon cutoff and begins to run through hummocks of thorn-studded mesquite. For the Valley's early Shoshone inhabitants, the mesquite beans were a dietary staple.

A small thicket of mesquite forms a lovely setting for the graves of Shorty Harris and Jim Dayton. Here, 13.2 miles from the highway, is where Dayton died in July 1899 on a trip from Furnace Creek to Dagget for supplies. It wasn't thirst that got him. When his body was found curled up under the mesquite, his wagon was close by with brakes set and plenty of water in the barrels. Dayton had been ill, and the crushing July heat was too much for his weakened condition. The mules died of thirst in their traces.

Frank "Shorty" Harris was one of Death Valley's most colorful mining characters and an early friend of Dayton's. Although Shorty died in Big Pine in 1934, he'd requested that he be buried in Death Valley next to his old friend Dayton. And so he was, beneath the epitaph he'd penned for himself: "Here lies Shorty Harris, a single blanket jackass prospector."

Half a mile south of the graves is the site of the Eagle Borax Works, Death Valley's first borax operation. Eagle Borax is one of Death Valley's many tales of high hopes and broken dreams. Fifty men worked here collecting "cottonball"— clusters of crystallized borates that grow on the surface—from the surrounding marshlands. After it was boiled in a giant vat, the low-grade product was hauled to market in a 12-mule-team wagon. Plagued by several problems, heat not the least of them, the borax works shut down in 1884 after two years of operation. Only 130 tons of low-grade borax had been shipped. Facing bankruptcy, Eagle Borax's discoverer and owner, Isadore Daunet, committed suicide.

Today there is little evidence of mining activity to see here. Nevertheless, Eagle Borax is worth a visit for its singular view of the Black Mountains rising from behind a broad green tule swamp, and the soft background music of crickets and songbirds.

Three miles south of Eagle Borax is Bennett's Well, marked by a stand of mesquite and a California State Historical Marker. At this site in 1849, the Bennett and Arcan families, disillusioned and suffering from scurvy and starvation, waited for 26 torturous days while William Manly and John Rogers hiked to civilization to bring back aid. Like much of Death Valley history, however, the facts are clouded by uncertainty. Some believe, based on Manly's later writings, that the actual location of the camp was at Eagle Borax Spring or even 3 miles farther north at Tule Spring.

Beyond Bennett's Well the road is generally more deteriorated. If you have any doubt about your vehicle's capabilities, you may want to retrace your route from this point.

West Side Road provides access to the main canyons on the east face of the Panamint Range. All require four-wheel drive. Well-marked roads lead to the five canyons, which are, from north to south, Trail Canyon (24-mile round trip); Hanaupah Canyon (16-mile round trip); Johnson Canyon (20-mile round trip); Galena Canyon (11-mile round trip); and Butte Valley (42-mile round trip). Detailed information on these canyons is available at the Visitor Center.

3

STOVEPIPE WELLS AREA

The windswept edge of a sand dune on the center of Death Valley's baking floor.... A more unlikely spot to find water can hardly be imagined. Yet here, more than a hundred years ago, water was discovered—good drinkable water close to the surface. For many years the two shallow, hand-dug water holes here were marked for thirsty travelers by a double length of iron stove pipe. Thus the name, Stovepipe Well.

In the 1920s, Death Valley's first tourist resort was almost built at the wells. But the lumber-hauling trucks from Lone Pine, which rolled on hard-rubber tires, couldn't get traction on the soft sand of the Valley floor, so the building materials were unloaded 4.5 miles west of the wells. It was there the bungalow city was constructed, and despite the shortfall, the developer named it Stovepipe Wells Hotel. Today it is known as Stovepipe Wells Village.

All the destinations in this chapter are within an hour of Stovepipe, as Death Valley regulars call the area. Visiting the sites will require a full day, although Titus Canyon itself can easily be an all-day trip for the leisurely visitor with time to picnic and explore. A suggested itinerary is to visit the locations in the order presented here, starting at Harmony Borax and winding up the day with sunset on the sand dunes followed by dinner and socializing at Stovepipe Wells Village.

HARMONY BORAX

1.5 miles north of the Visitor Center on Highway 190. Map on page 17.

As a mineral, borax lacks the romance of gold and silver. It is a utilitarian substance, used in such mundane applications as soaps, fertilizers, insecticides, and fiberglass. But unglamorous though it may be, borax has been the life blood of Death Valley's mining industry since the 1880s.

Harmony Borax Works was built in 1882. Located on a picturesque hillside, the tiny industrial operation overlooked Cottonball Marsh, a vast salt flat stretching to the north and west. Laborers gathered the "cottonball" and carted it to Harmony where the borates were boiled in water with soda. The resulting solution was run into large settling tanks and then transferred to smaller tanks where it crystal-

Opposite: The dunes are most dramatic in early morning or late afternoon light. LEWIS KEMPER *Below: A few adobe walls remain from the original Harmony Borax Works.* MARK J. DOLYAK

Top: The borax wagons had 7-foot-high wheels and could carry 10 tons each. GEORGE WUERTHNER
Bottom: A 20-mule team is hitched up at Harmony Borax Works in the 1880s. NATIONAL PARK SERVICE
Right: Mustard Canyon derives its name from the area's yellow mudstones. LONDIE G. PADELSKY

lized onto iron rods.

At the site today you can see the crumbling adobe remains of several buildings as well as a huge boiler and a pair of dissolving tanks, part of the original equipment by which the borate deposits were reduced to market–ready borax. A stroll through Harmony, with its interpretive signs and old photographs, gives a good thumbnail history of the borax mining industry.

Also on display here are the giant wagons that carried Harmony's product to the railhead at Mojave, 165 miles to the south. These wagons, their 7-foot-high wheels bound in quarter-ton iron tires, were drawn by the famous 20-mule teams. (Actually there were nine teams of mules and one team of draft horses at the rear to "horse" the wagon tongue around on the turns.) The normal rig was two wagons of borax and a 1,200-gallon water tank: a total load of more than 36 tons, of which 20 tons were payload.

Driving the wagons was a tricky process. An early guidebook described how the animals were controlled "by profanity and a cotton jerk line." On tight turns, the middle mule teams had to jump over a chain that ran down the length of the train. They then pulled in opposition to the turning lead mules—making sure that the wagon went around the curve rather than across it—before jumping back to the other side.

Unwieldy as the system sounds, it was efficient. From 1883 to 1888, 20 million

pounds of borax were shipped by mule team, with no reported breakdowns of the wagons.

At the north end of the works, an unsigned trail heads northwest toward the salt flats where the borax was gathered. At the end of this often wet and messy hike are the "haystacks," 10 square miles of borate piles stacked by Chinese laborers in the 1880s to prove mining claim assess–ment work. The round trip hike is about 5 miles, so carry extra water.

Leaving the parking lot at Harmony Borax, turn left (away from Highway 190) for an interesting 1.3-mile drive through Mustard Canyon. The one-way dirt road winds between fractured yellow mudstone walls frosted with white salt crystals. In late afternoon or early morning, stop and listen for odd creaking and popping sounds as the hills expand and contract.

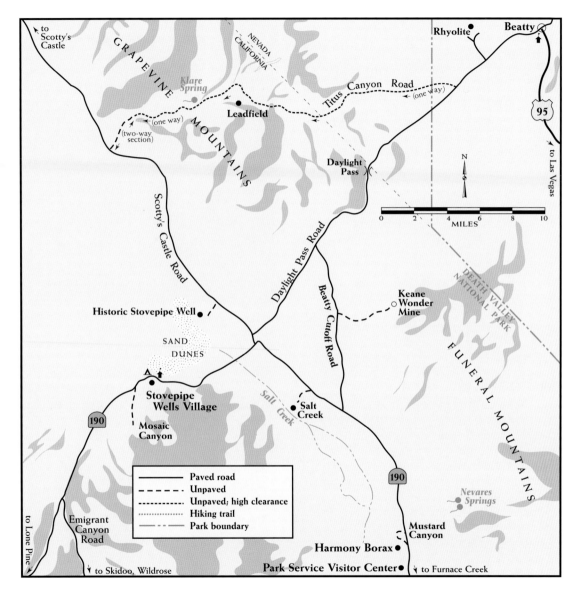

SALT CREEK

14 miles north of the Visitor Center via Highway 190. A gravel road leads west 1.2 miles to a parking area with picnic tables and a vault toilet. Map on this page.

Darting about in the shallows of Salt Creek, the Salt Creek pupfish (less than 2 inches long) seem small and fragile. Their life is not easy. Most get trapped in drying puddles in the spring and early summer, and only a lucky few access the deeper pools that last throughout summer. Many are eaten by the ravens and killdeer that congregate here, and by the occasional great blue heron.

Looked at from an evolutionary perspective, however, the little critters are perhaps the toughest in Death Valley. When 90-mile-long, freshwater Lake Manly shrank to nothing, it left this infinitesimally smaller trickle of water that is as salty as the ocean. No one knows

The Salt Creek pupfish is one of several rare desert fishes in Death Valley National Park. TOM MYERS

how many species of fish and amphibians disappeared in that process, but the pupfish adapted and survived. This particular species, the Salt Creek pupfish, exists nowhere else in the world.

A boardwalk zigzags on a half–mile tour of Salt Creek, meandering through a sea of pickleweed and salt grass while the creek threads in and out, now on one side, now the other, a mere trickle here, a pool there. Interpretive signs on the boardwalk will answer your questions about this strange stream of saltwater flowing quietly through the desert.

TITUS CANYON

35 miles north of the Visitor Center. Leave the Park via Daylight Pass Road. If you are coming from the Visitor Center, the Beatty Cutoff Road is a good shortcut from Highway 190 to Daylight Pass. On the left-hand side of Daylight Pass Road, 2.7 miles past the Park boundary, is Titus Canyon Road, which runs one way from east to west. It is 27 miles long and connects with the Scotty's Castle Road about 15 miles north of Highway 190. Titus Canyon Road may be closed due to weather, so check at the Visitor Center or with a ranger for current conditions. A high-clearance vehicle is recommended. Map on page 17.

In its 12–mile length, Titus Canyon serves up a varied menu: spectacular scenery, the remains of a town spawned by a mining scam, a comprehensive lesson in geology, Native American petroglyphs, and—if you're lucky—a glimpse of rare desert bighorn sheep. The canyon can be a great educational experience. More than that, it is breathtakingly beautiful.

The winding floor of Titus Canyon traverses the longest and deepest narrows in Death Valley, twisting between sheer rock faces hundreds of feet high. This is the drive that will make you wish you'd bought a convertible—and maybe make you nervous about flash floods!

Access to the canyon is roundabout. You leave the Park through Daylight Pass, heading east toward Beatty, Nevada. On the left, shortly after the "Welcome To Nevada" sign, Titus Canyon Road cuts

Above: Fortunate visitors sometimes spot bighorn sheep in Titus Canyon. RICK McINTYRE
Left: Salt Creek supports an unusual desert ecosystem. LYNN RADEKA

back in the direction you came. At this point you are just a couple of miles shy of the turn–of–the–century mining town of Rhyolite with its famous bottle house—well worth a side trip. You are also in sight of an unbelievably large 1990s–style cyanide–leaching gold operation.

About a mile along Titus Canyon Road you cross the faint trace of a road running southwest. Old Dinah, the steam tractor at the entrance to Furnace

Creek Ranch, used to haul supplies on this road from Rhyolite to the Keane Wonder Mine.

For the first dozen miles Titus Canyon Road ambles west across the Amargosa Valley. Then it crests the Grape-vine Mountains at Red Pass and tilts toward the floor of Death Valley. Another 3 miles of driving brings you to Leadfield. The town site was laid out in 1927 by a mining promoter, who also built Titus Canyon Road as part of what can most charitably be called an enthusiastic stock promotion.

Based on 14 low-grade lead claims and lots of hype, Leadfield drew eager prospectors and businessmen who built a booming mining town practically over-night. The real money lay not in lead but in stock sales, which netted the promoter about $1.5 million before the company went bust the same year. Several buildings remain as monuments to the avarice and gullibility of the times.

Down canyon 2.5 miles is Klare Springs, where you may see desert big-horn sheep come to water. The springs are also the site of early Native American petroglyphs, human and animal figures and geometric designs pecked into the rock surface. Sadly, the most accessible of the Klare Springs petroglyphs have been badly vandalized.

Below Klare Springs you enter the final stretch of the canyon, 4 miles of the most spectacular narrows accessible by road Death Valley has to offer. The

Above: On its descent towards Death Valley, Titus Canyon Road takes visitors through a deep, scenic gorge. MARK J. DOLYAK
Right: The historic gold-mining town of Rhyolite lies just east of the Park. LYNN RADEKA

walls soar hundreds of feet above the canyon floor, which narrows at one point to less than 20 feet wide. Then suddenly you exit the canyon onto a huge alluvial fan. From here to the high-way (about 3 miles) you are again on a two-way road.

Above: Desert winds create an ever-changing ripple pattern on the Death Valley dunes. GEORGE WARD
Right: A beetle leaves its delicate tracks on the dunes.
DANIEL D'AGOSTINI

SAND DUNES

Drive about 23 miles north and west of the visitor Center on Highway 190 to a wide pullout and an interpretive sign on the right hand side. The sand dunes can be accessed from here; this route is the most common way to walk out to the dunes. Map on page 17.

The sand dunes are the most purely fun place in Death Valley. People from not-so-near desert towns such as Ridgecrest routinely drive for hours to Death Valley on a weekend just to play in the dunes. Romping on the sand is usually the part of a Death Valley vacation that young people remember best.

You can walk anywhere on the dunes. Give in to temptation and take off your shoes early. Many people like to climb to the highest point of the highest dune, a feat best undertaken from the interpretive sign on Highway 190.

The sand dunes are one of the few places in a national park where you don't have to be concerned about leaving tracks. The wind, nature's great eraser, periodically cleans them away.

That same wind built and is still building the dunes. Laden with sand picked up as it blows through the Valley (sometimes in excess of 80 miles per hour), the wind runs into Tucki Mountain, a nearly 7,000-foot peak whose slopes jut into the Valley south of Stovepipe. The mountain causes back-eddies that slow the airflow, allowing the sand to drop to the ground. The air currents are slowest above the eastern end of the dunes, and that's where the smallest particles settle out.

Two words of caution. Anything dropped onto the sand disappears almost instantaneously and is nearly impossible to find. Don't put the car keys in your pocket if you're going to be rolling down hills or turning handsprings. Second, the sand is extremely fine and gets into everything. This is particularly true if you are with kids. It's best to carry your camera—and anything else you don't want "sanded"—in a tightly sealed bag. A plastic sack with the top twisted shut will do.

If you leave your camera in the car, you'll regret it, because the play of light and shade on the dunes creates fantastic photo opportunities at any time of day. When viewing the dunes from Highway 190, sunset and the first light of daybreak create the best effects.

If you travel on the dirt access road at the eastern end of the dunes, you'll

come to the original Stovepipe Well. Just before that on the right is the grave of Val Nolan, "Victim of the Elements," at the spot where his body was found and buried by a motion picture crew in 1931.

STOVEPIPE WELLS VILLAGE

24 miles north and west of the Visitor Center via Highway 190. Map on page 17.

Death Valley has long attracted people with dreams and schemes. Bob Eichbaum's plan fell in both categories. In 1925 and 1926 he built a 38–mile toll road from Panamint Valley across Towne Pass to Stovepipe Wells. Almost to the original Stovepipe Well, anyway. The sand stopped him a few miles short. The Death Valley Toll Road opened in 1926 at a cost of $2 per car and 50¢ per occupant.

At the Death Valley end of the toll road, not surprisingly, were Eichbaum's 20 newly constructed bungalows containing 50 rooms: the Stovepipe Wells Hotel. To boost tourism, Eichbaum started a "stage line" to haul visitors to Death Valley from Los Angeles in Studebaker Phaetons.

Today Stovepipe Wells Village offers a full range of amenities to the desert–weary traveler: a campground and RV hookups, motel, swimming pool, airstrip, gas station, general store and gift shop, restaurant, and ranger station. And, of course, there's the Badwater Saloon, to cut the dust.

Immediately west of the village on Highway 190, a gravel road climbs an alluvial fan toward massive Tucki Mountain. In 2.4 miles the road reaches the mouth of Mosaic Canyon. From there it's an easy quarter–mile hike into Mosaic's twisting narrows, with more beyond, if you're adventurous and a good climber.

Most striking is the rock itself. The same featureless, drab brown rock that makes up the mountain—marble and breccia, jagged rock fragments cemented together—has been transformed into sensuous undulating curves with a glowing, polished surface. The agent of this artistry is water–borne sediment that courses through the serpentine canyon during desert rainstorms.

Left: A short hike takes you to scenic narrows in lower Mosaic Canyon. ROBERT PARKER
Above: The scoured walls of Mosaic Canyon exhibit the artful pattern of their namesake rock formations. DENNIS FLAHERTY

4

NORTHERN DEATH VALLEY

The north end of Death Valley offers something for everyone. And it is also big! A round trip from the Visitor Center to the locations described in this chapter involves about 200 miles of driving, and almost half of it is over rough gravel roads. Here, you are getting into some of the Park's more remote and rugged areas.

Although you can see Scotty's Castle, Ubehebe Crater, and the Eureka dunes in one long day, you'll get more out of your visit if you spend two or three days. In a single day, you can explore the astonishing artistry, architecture, and memorabilia at Scotty's Castle and also wend your way down the steep sides of 500-foot-deep Ubehebe Crater. The 49-mile stretch of gravel road from the Ubehebe Crater road to Eureka dunes is time consuming, but well worth the effort. You can easily spend an entire day playing at the Eureka dunes and struggling to the top its 700-foot-high ridge.

SCOTTY'S CASTLE ROAD

17.3 miles north of the Visitor Center via Highway 190. Just after 190 veers left toward the sand dunes, Scotty's Castle Road turns off to the right. Map on page 25.

From its southern terminus at Highway 190 to Scotty's Castle, 36 miles farther north, Scotty's Castle Road traces the edge of the Grapevine Mountains. Across the floor of the Valley to your left are the Cottonwood Mountains. At Highway 190, the two ranges are separated by a distance of about 18 miles, but they converge north of Scotty's Castle to form the north end of Death Valley proper.

About 2.5 miles north of Highway 190, pull over at the monument titled "Wagon Wheel History." On both sides of the road you can see old wagon tracks, probably made by the repair wagons that serviced the Rhyolite–Skidoo telegraph lines. A few hundred feet farther along the

highway, a dirt road on the left leads downhill toward the original Stovepipe Well and the dunes. On the right at 11.5 miles is a geological interpretive display at the foot of a precipitous alluvial fan. This steep and heavily gullied mass of rubble pouring from the canyon mouth is typical of the alluvial fans in the Grapevine Mountains. The road turns suddenly west

Opposite: Past episodes of volcanic activity spewed lava over parts of Eureka Valley. JIM STIMSON
Below: Scotty's Castle. MARK J. DOLYAK

a couple of miles farther on, and directly ahead of you across the Valley is Dry Bone Canyon. Compare its broad, gently sloped alluvial fan with the one you just left.

The turnoff for the west end of Titus Canyon is 14.7 miles up Scotty's Castle Road from Highway 190. The 6-mile round trip to the canyon mouth is well worth your time. From the parking area, you can stroll into the splendid narrows of Titus Canyon (see Chapter 3). Hike as far up as you like, but keep an ear out for vehicles

The Moorish-style complex known as Scotty's Castle was the 1930s vacation retreat of a wealthy Chicago couple. JEFF GNASS

on the narrow, winding, one-way road coming down the canyon from the east. In the gray rock to the right of the canyon entrance, low to the ground, look for petroglyphs. These designs were pecked into the rock by Native Americans hundreds, or perhaps thousands, of years ago.

Back on the highway, you'll notice the road begins to climb as it more closely hugs the Grapevine Mountains. The Cottonwood Mountains gradually crowd in on the left for the next 18 miles as you approach the north end of the Valley. Shortly past the turnoff to Mesquite Springs Campground, you reach Grapevine Ranger Station, where all vehicles must stop. You'll be asked to pay the Park entrance fee here, if you have not already done so at the Visitor Center.

Half a mile past the ranger station, the road splits. Turning to the left, it's 5.3 miles to Ubehebe Crater. The right fork takes you 3 miles to Scotty's Castle.

SCOTTY'S CASTLE

53 miles north of the Visitor Center via Highway 190 and Scotty's Castle Road. Veer right 0.6 mile north of Grapevine Ranger Station. Map on page 25.

The first indication that you are approaching Scotty's Castle is a line of concrete fence posts set 15 feet apart, paralleling the left side of the road. Look closely: cast into the side of each post near the bottom are the initials S and J, each in a circle, the S above the J. The S stands for Walter

Scott—"Death Valley Scotty"—a flamboyant prospector and mine promoter with less flair for finding rich strikes than for finding wealthy backers. The J stands for Albert Johnson, a shy, wealthy insurance man from Chicago.

Johnson initially bankrolled Scotty in 1904 to develop a supposed hidden gold mine in Death Valley. But long after it must have become clear to Johnson that he himself was Scotty's gold mine, he continued to supply money for Scotty's "mining" projects. The two became fast friends, and Johnson began to visit Death Valley regularly.

Soon Johnson's wife, Bessie, joined him on these trips. It was she who suggested they build a vacation home in Death Valley. They purchased the land—14,000 of those concrete fence posts mark the 10-mile perimeter boundary of the property—and construction began in 1922. By 1931, Johnson had invested $2 million in a sprawling Moorish-style complex that he called Death Valley Ranch and the rest of the world called Scotty's Castle.

With its massive hand-carved beams, red tiled roof, and 270-foot-long swimming pool, Scotty's Castle would make a striking impression in any location. But at 3,000 feet elevation in Grapevine Canyon, the Castle presents a truly spectacular sight against the dry rugged hills. As

The Moorish-style complex known as Scotty's Castle was the 1930s vacation retreat of a wealthy Chicago couple. JEFF GNASS

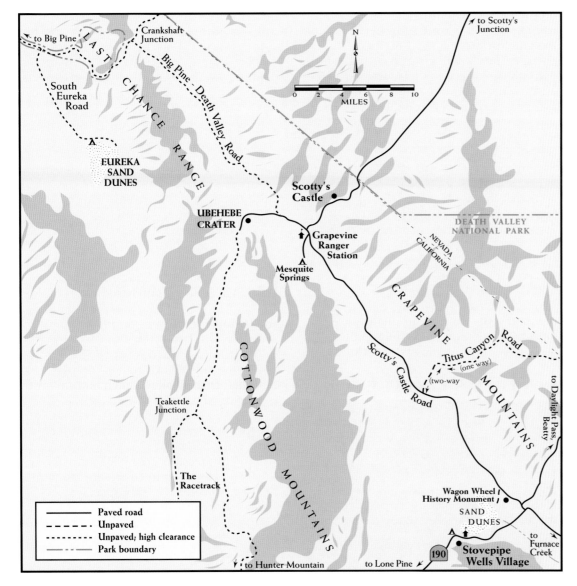

to Big Pine ←
Crankshaft Junction
to Scotty's Junction ↗

LAST CHANCE RANGE

Big Pine – Death Valley Road

South Eureka Road

N

0 2 4 6 8 10
MILES

EUREKA SAND DUNES

Scotty's Castle •

UBEHEBE CRATER •

DEATH VALLEY NATIONAL PARK

Grapevine Ranger Station

NEVADA
CALIFORNIA

Mesquite Springs

GRAPEVINE MOUNTAINS

Scotty's Castle Road

Titus Canyon Road
(one way)
(two-way)

COTTONWOOD MOUNTAINS

Teakettle Junction

to Daylight Pass, Beatty

The Racetrack

Wagon Wheel History Monument •

SAND DUNES

Paved road
- - - **Unpaved**
····· **Unpaved; high clearance**
—·— **Park boundary**

190 • Stovepipe Wells Village

to Furnace Creek

↑ to Hunter Mountain   to Lone Pine ↙

interesting as the overall spectacle, however, are its thousand-and-one details, from the prospector-and-burro weathervane atop the Main House to the 1,100-pipe Welte-Mignon theater organ in the Upper Music Room.

Throughout the day, Park Service personnel conduct "living history" tours of the Castle. The guides' speech, clothing, and the "current events" they discuss contribute to the impression that these folks walked straight out of the 1930s.

Scotty himself didn't live at the Castle. His far-more-modest home lies near Grapevine Springs, a few miles to the west. But it was Scotty who put the Castle on the map, visiting often and entertaining the Johnsons' guests, including the likes of Betty Grable and Will Rogers, in the Castle's Great Hall.

Scotty died in 1954 and is buried next to his dog, Windy, on a hill behind the Castle. The easy three-quarter-mile round-trip walk to the site takes you past the Castle's 1929 solar water heater and gives you a peek into Tie Canyon. The canyon got its name in 1928, after Johnson bought 120,000 railroad ties (70 miles of the abandoned Bullfrog Goldfield Railroad) for $1,500. The ties were to provide firewood for the Castle's 14 fireplaces. It cost Johnson $25,000 to move the ties to the canyon.

The picnic area in front of the Main House consists of 2 acres of well-maintained green lawn shaded by towering cottonwoods, a perfect place for the kids to work off a little steam. Youngsters should not, however, be left unsupervised. A spring-fed stream runs along the far side of the picnic area, and elsewhere on the grounds are more traditional desert dangers such as rattlesnakes (rarely) and cholla cactus. A snack bar, gift shop, restrooms, and two gas pumps—regular unleaded only—are located close to the picnic area.

Below left: Magma-heated groundwater exploded to the surface to form Ubehebe Crater. FRANK S. BALTHIS
Below right: Dawn light casts a rosy tint over the lakebed of the Racetrack. JIM STIMSON
Opposite: Due to their ability to capture and retain moisture, the Eureka dunes support a surprising variety of plants, including the endemic Eureka dunegrass (shown). GEORGE WARD

Scotty's Castle was never finished. Crates of hand-painted tiles today gather dust in the Main House basement; the bottom of the pool wasn't poured. But the Castle is a magnificent monument to Death Valley Scotty, a true Western legend. It is also a testimony to the curious friendship of two very different men, each of whom seems to have found in the other something missing in himself.

UBEHEBE CRATER

56 miles north of the Visitor Center via Highway 190 and Scotty's Castle Road. From Grapevine Ranger Station continue northwest (left) 5.9 miles to the parking area. Map on page 25.

As you approach Ubehebe Crater, the ground darkens. The landscape takes on an otherworldly appearance. You sense there is something strange ahead.

About 2,000 years ago, a huge chamber of magma—molten rock—was bulging upwards far beneath this spot, working its way toward the surface. Then it met groundwater, millions of gallons

percolating downward through the earth. In an instant, the water flashed to steam and a horrendous explosion blew a hole more than 500 feet deep and half a mile wide through the overlaying fanglomerate (old alluvial fans hardened into rock). Volcanic cinder spewed upward and outward, covering an area of several square miles.

From the viewing area, the cinder layer is clearly seen as a gray frosting atop the orange fanglomerate on the far side. Much of the cinder material has eroded back down into the crater in sheets.

Hiking down into the crater is fun and deceptively easy. The hike back up the 30° slope, however, can be taxing.

A slightly less strenuous hike begins at the parking area and follows the right edge of the crater rim. Because of the steepness of the crater wall, keep children away from the edge of the trail. In half a mile of sometimes steep hiking you reach Little Hebe Crater, a miniature of Ubehebe. Little Hebe, Ubehebe, and half a dozen similar craters in the area are what geologists call Maar craters.

Beyond Ubehebe Crater 28 miles on a high-clearance road (take the right fork at Teakettle Junction), lies the Racetrack. One of the most mysterious and remote regions of Death Valley, the Racetrack is best known for its "moving rocks." Hefty boulders somehow travel across the dry lake bed–moved by high winds when the playa is slick with a chance rainstorm or icy mud, perhaps?– leaving clear tracks of their journey.

EUREKA SAND DUNES

98 miles north of the Visitor Center via Highway 190, Scotty's Castle Road, Big Pine-Death Valley Road, and South Eureka Road. The last 45 miles are on rough dirt road that begins 3.4 miles north of Grapevine Ranger Station and 2.5 miles east of Ubehebe Crater. Coming from Big Pine, travel 50 miles via Highway 168, Big Pine-Death Valley Road, and South Eureka Road. Map on page 25.

Under normal conditions, driving the 45 miles of dirt road (with intermittent short stretches of pavement) from Scotty's Castle Road to Eureka sand dunes takes about two hours. Check road conditions at Scotty's Castle or the Visitor Center before leaving. For the first 20 miles you travel up the wide, flat, northernmost end of Death Valley with the Last Chance Range on your left. Resist the temptation to speed up on this straight stretch—deep, tooth-jarring ruts appear as if out of nowhere.

After Crankshaft Junction, you climb into the Last Chance Range. The views are exciting, but keep your eyes on the narrow, twisting road. After 10 miles you begin to drop into Eureka Valley. Shortly after you reach the valley floor, the access road to the dunes cuts off to the left.

Geologists describe the dunes in terms like seif, aeolian, and loess. But for the lay person, these massive ridges of sand are simply stupendous. The highest dune towers 664 to 700 feet above the playa floor (measurements vary), making it the highest dune in California. The dunes' subtly changing color and graceful form

are particularly dramatic when viewed against the wildly colored, jaggedly banded Last Chance Range.

The 4,300-acre Eureka dunes have been described as an ecological island. The adjacent Last Chance Range forces clouds upwards, wringing out extra moisture so slightly more rain and snow fall here than on other dune fields in the Park. This moisture, combined with the age of the dunes – they are almost 10,000 years old – results in abundant plant and animal life. More than 50 species of plants are found in the system, three of them endemic. Most well-known of these is Eureka Dune Grass. Brown-stemmed with bright green, sword-shaped leaves, it forms tufted hummocks on the flanks of the dunes.

The Eureka dunes are a success story, but barely. By the 1970s, they had become a playground for off-road vehicles. Under pressure from environmentalists, the dunes became a National Natural Landmark in 1983. Then in 1994, 200,000-acre Eureka Valley became part of the newly designated Death Valley National Park, with the level of protection accorded only the nation's most unique and valuable natural resources. Visitors are urged to tread gently in this environmentally fragile zone. The hummocks of dunegrass have still not fully recovered from vehicle impact.

Finally, the Eureka dunes are singing dunes. Hikers on the high ridges will sometimes hear a humming similar to a bass violin or the lower notes of a pipe

organ. Several variables are involved in this phenomenon, including the moisture content of the dunes and the grain shape and surface texture of the sand. But for desert lovers, the song of the dunes is a mystery that doesn't need a solution.

5
WILDROSE AND THE HIGH COUNTRY

In 1860, a group of silver seekers from Visalia, California, under the leadership of Dr. Samuel G. George, set out to search for Death Valley's fabled Lost Gunsight lode. They entered the Panamint Range, that massive dividing wall between Panamint Valley and Death Valley, through an inviting canyon on the west side. Midway up the canyon they found a heavily flowing spring that they named for the wild roses that grew thick there.

One of the party climbed the highest peak in the area and on returning exclaimed to his partners that only through a telescope had he ever before seen so far! The peak was promptly named Telescope Peak and shortly thereafter the Telescope Mining District was organized.

George's party didn't find the Lost Gunsight. But the lure of precious metals brought other prospectors, and soon the high country of the Panamints, from Tucki Mountain in the north to Butte Valley in the south, was ringing with the sound of pick and shovel. As high-paying ore was discovered, those sounds were replaced with the booming of dynamite, crashing of stamp mills, and creaking of heavy, ore-laden wagons. Millions of dollars in gold and silver, in the form of dust, bars, and ingots, flowed from the Panamints to the nation's centers of commerce.

In this part of your Death Valley visit you'll experience the mining legacy of the Panamints and see some spectacular views of Death Valley. Late May through October are the best times to visit. The coolness (elevations range from 5,600 feet at Skidoo to 11,049 feet atop Telescope Peak) is a much welcome counterpoint to the 120°+ summer temperatures on the Valley floor.

Opposite: In the 1870s, Wildrose Canyon kilns reduced pinyon pine to charcoal for ore smelters in the adjacent Argus Range. DENNIS FLAHERTY *Right: The Skidoo Mill is perched high in the Panamint Range.* TOM TILL

SKIDOO

44 miles from the Visitor Center. Follow Highway 190 north and west to Emigrant Canyon Road, 9 miles west of Stovepipe Wells Village. Take Emigrant Canyon Road south 9.5 miles to Skidoo Road on the left. This dirt road leads 7.2 miles to the Skidoo site. Use extreme caution in areas of old mine sites. Map on page 36.

Above: This tunnel is one of the few remnants of a short-lived mining camp at Harrisburg, named after legendary prospector Shorty Harris. ERIC WUNROW
Opposite: The Panamint's Aguereberry Point offers a view to rival any in the Park. ERIC WUNROW

What is perhaps most remarkable about the site of Skidoo is how little there is to see at first glance. Topping a ridge about 7 miles from the highway, you enter a small, empty, bowl-shaped valley. Had you done that in 1907, you'd have been driving into a town that boasted 130 homes and businesses and 500 citizens. In the hills around Skidoo miners feverishly dug gold-rich ore from more than 1,000 mine shafts and tunnels. Yet today, virtually nothing remains of the town itself save for scattered bits of metal, wood, and glass. The surrounding mine workings have fared better, however, and offer an excellent opportunity for a cautious adult to explore many aspects of the mineral-extraction process.

It is commonly believed that the bustling boomtown of Skidoo was named by Bob Montgomery's wife. In 1906, not long after he sold another mine for a million dollars, Bob purchased 23 highly promising claims from two men who, lost in the fog, had literally stumbled on the fabulous gold find. When he told Winnie Montgomery of his purchase, she is said to have responded "23 Skidoo," a popular vaudevillian phrase of the day. The name caught on, and though Bob formally named his new town Montgomery, it was known to the rest of the world simply as Skidoo. Other folks maintain that the name Skidoo relates to the length of an iron pipeline, an engineering marvel that supplied water for the town's milling operation. But that pipeline to Skidoo

from Birch Springs, near Telescope Peak, was only 21 miles long, and postdates the town's name. The pipe was sold for its iron value during World War I.

The best place to start exploring is at the Skidoo Mill, a 25-stamp operation that in its ten-year production life processed more than $1.3 million in gold at $20 an ounce. Drive 1.2 miles north from the Skidoo interpretive signs, taking the right fork to the road closure gate. Then it's a 600-foot walk to the 25-stamp mill. Beyond the mill to the north is a splendid vista spanning Tucki Mountain and the Valley floor west of Stovepipe. From the mill, wander through the hills and inspect the scattered mining ruins, being especially cautious of rotten wood in mining structures and loose rock. On a hot day, you can relax in the mouth of one of the longer tunnels, from which chill breezes constantly flow. Be sure to carry water.

AGUEREBERRY POINT

Follow Emigrant Canyon Road 2.4 miles south of Skidoo Road to Aguereberry Point Road on the left. A high-clearance vehicle is recommended for the drive to Aguereberry Point. Map on page 36.

Two years before the Skidoo boom and just 5 miles to the south, a tent city grew nearly overnight near a low hill that rises from what is now Harrisburg Flat. The story began at Furnace Creek in July 1905. Famed Death Valley prospector Shorty Harris (see Chapter 2), freshly grub-staked, was looking for a partner. He tied in with

Aguereberry Point parking lot. Then, for the best possible vantage point, walk to the far left side of the parking lot, left of the large blocky outcropping, and follow the path east for 250 yards. At the end you see Death Valley as if you were suspended in a basket above it. The drop to the Valley is steep, and the feeling is vertiginous. Keep children close.

Binoculars help here, but even with the naked eye you can see the dark green mesquite surrounding Furnace Creek. Also visible are the date palm groves and even the red roofs of Furnace Creek Inn. Past that, behind the Amargosa Range that fences the east side of Death Valley, the desert mountain ranges march into Nevada and the blue-gray horizon.

a Basque miner named Jean Pierre "Pete" Aguereberry (the Basque pronunciation is "a-gear-a-berry"), and the pair set off for the cooler high country to prospect. They happened on a gold-rich ledge, hiked on to Ballarat in Panamint Valley to file their claims, and then raced back up Wildrose Canyon to fend off claim jumpers.

Within two months, hundreds of miners were working around the hill where the pair had made their strike. The town of Harrisburg sprang up—not much of a town by the standards of the day, only one saloon—then faded within a year. As the gold played out, most of the miners moved on. But old Pete kept on working his Eureka Mine until he died in 1945.

On the right 1.5 miles along Aguereberry Point Road is the site of Pete Aguereberry's camp, snug against the hill that held his gold. The several structures date from Aguereberry's occupancy, and their haphazard mix of building materials and techniques are typical of many small Western mining camps. From the buildings, walk east past an ancient bullet-riddled Buick and around the end of the hill to the Eureka Mine. You'll want a flashlight to explore here. Other mining remains litter the hill.

Past the camp another 4.7 miles you suddenly come to a breathtaking view of Death Valley. But that is not quite "the Grand View," as Pete called it. Continue along the ridge for another 0.4 mile to the

CHARCOAL KILNS

Follow Emigrant Canyon Road 16.4 miles south and then east from Aguereberry Point Road to the charcoal kilns. Because of the road's narrowness and curves, you'll need to slow to 10 miles per hour in places. At the 9-mile point you come to Wildrose Spring, marked by a profusion of willows, and the right-hand turnoff of the Trona-Wildrose Road, which leads into Panamint Valley. Keep to the left, and just beyond the spring you pass the old Wildrose Ranger Station and Campground. After the road begins to climb, you cross the Skidoo pipeline route. The spot is marked with a Park Service interpretive display on the left. Map on page 36.

Skidoo, Harrisburg, and the other mining towns of the Panamint Range are

newcomers compared to the Wildrose charcoal kilns. These ten rock–and–mortar monuments to American ingenuity date from around 1875, when local precious–metals mining was facing a crisis.

In the Argus Range, on the west side of Panamint Valley, the Minnietta and Modock mines were producing huge amounts of silver ore. To free the silver from the native rock required smelting, a process that needs intense heat and carbon. No natural coal existed in the Argus Range, nor did any trees grow there that could be processed into charcoal.

Across Panamint Valley to the east, however, in the soaring Panamint Range, pinyon pines covered the slopes at altitudes above 6,000 feet. To the west, a problem; to the east, a solution. By 1877 the Wildrose charcoal kilns had been built, and the western slopes of the Panamints were being logged to feed the kilns. Charcoal was shipped down Wildrose Canyon, across Panamint Valley, and up a tramway to the mines, a distance of 25 miles. Production at the kilns probably continued only until around 1879.

The kilns, each about 25 feet in height and 30 feet in diameter, have a surreal appearance. Although their shape is reminiscent of the onion tops of Russian Orthodox churches, they were designed strictly for efficiency and were constructed of raw slabs of local stone roughly mortared together. The parabolic shape that focused the heat, the top and bottom loading doors, and the air vents on the circumference of the kilns were all essential to the fine art of charcoal making. More than a week was required, under the eyes of a skilled charcoal maker, to convert the 42 cords of wood in a fully loaded kiln into about 2,100 bushels of charcoal.

Despite the crude materials and functional design, these structures have a grace and beauty all their own and are uniquely photographable and sketchable, both inside and out.

To appreciate the focusing effect of the parabolic interior, stand by the lower loading door, take a deep breath, and utter a moderately loud, continuous tone as you walk slowly to the center of the kiln. The near perfect geometry of the cone will gradually focus your sound until, as you reach the precise center, it sounds as if someone turned on the amplifiers. Children especially enjoy this and can be well entertained going from kiln to kiln comparing acoustics.

PEAK TRAILS: WILDROSE AND TELESCOPE

The Wildrose Peak trailhead is at the north (down-canyon) end of the Charcoal Kilns parking area. To reach the Telescope Peak trailhead, follow Mahogany Flat Road 1.8 miles south from the Charcoal Kilns. This road is steep and twisting, so check conditions with a ranger before attempting it in a two-wheel-drive vehicle. Map on page 36.

If you want an invigorating hiking experience but your time is somewhat limited, try the Wildrose Peak climb. You'll be rewarded with gorgeous views of Death Valley to the east and Panamint Valley to the west. The hike is 4.2 miles one way, and it climbs from 6,894 feet at the charcoal kilns to 9,064 feet at Wildrose Peak. The best views occur in the second half of the hike. Although this is not a particularly strenuous climb, the final mile of switchbacks up to the peak is quite steep; folks who live near sea level will find their breath coming shorter in the thin mountain air.

A more ambitious trek is the Telescope Peak Trail, a 14-mile round trip to the highest point in Death Valley National

Park. Allow a full day and leave as early in the morning as possible. The official trailhead, where you sign the trail guest book, is a few hundred feet south of the Mahogany Flat parking area. Except for roads for authorized emergency and maintenance vehicles, this is the highest point—8,133 feet above sea level—that can be driven to in the Park.

In the trail's first 2 miles you complete half of its 3,000-foot elevation gain. From there on the hiking is easier as you pass through the green sweep of Arcane Meadow (a good place to picnic) and enter ancient bristlecone pine country. The views encountered during this climb are truly splendid. It's easy to understand why a miner, John Thorndyke, once planned to open a hotel on the peak. He wound up instead with several tourist cabins at what is now Thorndike Campground.

As you hike the well-made and well-maintained trail, think about the young men of the Civilian Conservation Corps (CCC) who built the trail in the mid-1930s. Brought in from all over the country as part of President Roosevelt's program to fight the Great Depression, the young men of the CCC built campgrounds, wells, and hundreds of miles of roads in and around Death Valley. Several thousand square miles of California and Nevada—including the highest and lowest points in the lower 48 states—are visible with binoculars from atop Telescope Peak.

Late May to early June is the best time to take this hike, but it can be hiked any time during the summer and early fall. In late spring the snow has melted on the peak, but the heat haze from the Valley floor is not yet enough to affect the views into Death Valley.

Opposite: The rare Panamint daisy grows on the western slopes of the range. ANDY SELTERS
Right: During winter, the higher elevations of the Park are often dusted with snow. LYNN RADEKA
Below: The trail to Telescope Peak takes hikers past stands of ancient bristlecone pine and rewards them with incomparable vistas of the Park. ROBERT PARKER

6
PANAMINT
AND SALINE VALLEYS

When Death Valley National Monument became a National Park in 1994, among the major additions were northern Panamint Valley and Saline Valley. Both are similar to Death Valley in their geology, biology, and climate. Both share similar cultural histories: millennia of intermittent hunter–gatherer occupation followed by an influx of miners from the mid–nineteenth to the early twentieth century. At that point, however, the history of Death Valley diverged sharply from that of Panamint and Saline.

Tourism caught on in Death Valley in the 1920s. After the Valley was designated a National Monument in 1933, the number of visitors began to climb. By 1992 it had reached more than a million people per year.

Panamint and Saline valleys missed the tourist stream, and it shows. From the north end of Saline Valley to the south end of Panamint Valley—100 miles as the crow flies, closer to 150 by road—there is not a single public telephone. There is one gas station at Panamint Springs, and more road is unpaved than paved. There are no ranger, police, sheriff, or highway patrol stations. Here lies the true outback of Death Valley National Park.

PANAMINT VALLEY

54 miles from the Visitor Center via Highway 190 to Panamint Springs Resort on the western edge of the valley. From Lone Pine travel 48 miles on Highways 136 and 190. Map on page 36.

Winding westward down the steep grade into Panamint Valley, you'll catch glimpses of Lake Hill looming dark above the dry lake bed on the valley floor. A rest area 3.7 miles west of Towne Pass presents a good view and a chance to cool your brakes.

North of Lake Hill are the Panamint dunes, several square miles of sand on the upslope to Hunter Mountain at the north end of the valley. On the north side of Highway 190, 9.8 miles west of Towne Pass,

Opposite: Well-equipped desert explorers enjoy the solitude of Saline Valley. ANDY SELTERS
Below: Mound cactus add a dash of scarlet to rocky slopes near Panamint Valley. DENNIS FLAHERTY

is a dirt road that leads to Lake Hill and then passes within 3 miles of the dunes.

It is 11.7 miles west from Towne Pass to Panamint Valley Road and access to the south end of the valley, which is administer by the Bureau of Land Management (BLM). Worth a visit is the "ghost town" of Ballarat, a mining town that served the Panamint mines from 1897 to 1917. The 3-mile dirt road to Ballarat begins about 23 paved miles south of Highway 190. If you are interested in visiting these areas, the Ridgecrest office of the BLM has information on Ballarat, the Minnietta and Modock mines (see Chapter 5), and other south Panamint attractions.

Meandering down the east side of Panamint Valley is Wingate Road (dirt), which gives access to most of the canyons on this side of the Panamint Range. Hiking trips to sites such as Panamint City at the head of Surprise Canyon require experienced backcountry travelers with plenty of preparation. (The old road through Surprise Canyon has been closed.)

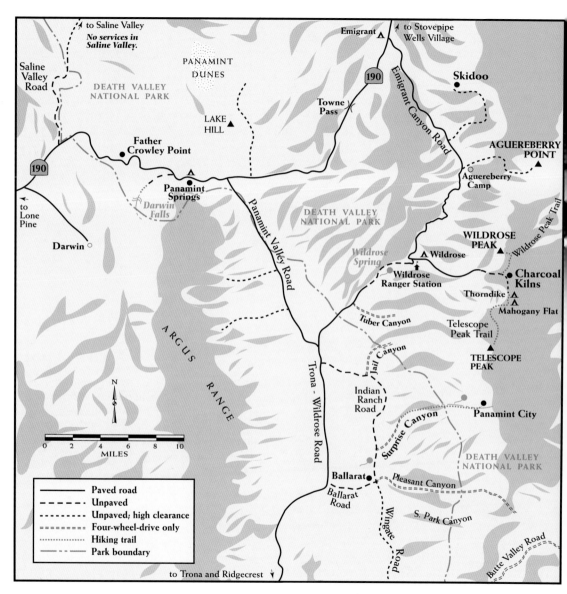

Legend:
- Paved road
- - - - Unpaved
- · · · Unpaved; high clearance
- = = = Four-wheel-drive only
- · · · · · Hiking trail
- — · — Park boundary

Continuing west on Highway 190 as it climbs out of Panamint Valley, you come to Panamint Springs Resort (14.3 miles west of Towne Pass). If you're heading to Saline Valley, this is a good place to stop to fill your gas tank and have a cold drink.

On the left, a mile west of the resort, is the cutoff to Darwin Falls. Follow the dirt road 2.4 miles, keeping right at the fork, to the parking area. A half-hour hike, with a few scrambles over rock and the possibility of muddy feet, brings you to a lovely cascading waterfall, 30 feet high, that flows year round. Listen for the laughlike, descending call of canyon wrens floating through the narrow canyon—one of more than 80 species of resident and migratory birds that frequent this tiny desert oasis.

Continuing west on Highway 190 you encounter an uphill, narrow, twisting stretch with steep drop-offs, not advised for faint-of-heart drivers or extra-wide vehicles. You reach Father Crowley Point 6.9 miles west of the Darwin Falls cutoff. Known as "the Desert Padre," Father Crowley was a Catholic priest who ministered throughout Inyo County in the 1930s and was the chaplain for the CCC boys in Death Valley. He is said to have frequently stopped to rest at this point. Close to the pullout is a great view of rugged Rainbow Canyon. Take the dirt road to the right of the parking area 0.6 mile for a glorious view of the Panamint dunes, Lake Hill, the banded cliffs of Panamint Butte, and Telescope Peak.

SALINE VALLEY

This trip requires a full gas tank, extra water, a detailed map, and high-clearance vehicle (sometimes 4x4—inquire about current conditions). From the Visitor Center, it is 68 miles on Highway 190 to the Saline Valley Road turnoff. Follow the road, bearing right at Lee Flat, 8.2 miles, to the fork at the head of Grapevine Canyon (15.6 miles); turn left to enter Saline Valley. It's another 60 miles from here to the junction with Big Pine-Death Valley Road, and then 15 additional miles to the nearest services on Highway 395 in Big Pine. Coming from Lone Pine, it is 34.6 miles via Highways 136 and 190 to Saline Valley Road. (A cutoff 27.6 miles from Lone Pine also connects to Saline Valley Road.) Map on page 39.

Above: Lee Flat, on the route to Saline Valley, supports a forest of Joshua trees. FRED HIRSCHMANN
Left: The enchanting cascade of Darwin Falls is accessible only on foot. JON STEWART
Opposite: This desert iguana in Saline Valley is at the northern edge of the range for the species. In warm months it is often seen near creosote bush, a principal food in its diet. MORGAN BALL/PLACE PHOTOGRAPHY

Turn off Highway 190 onto the Saline Valley Road. Take a deep breath, check your gas gauge, and mentally inventory your water supply. A long drive lies ahead.

Initially the road is wide and well groomed. At Lee Flat you pass through a Joshua tree forest that extends as far as the eye can see. Watch for cattle that are inclined to wander into the road.

The precipitous 10-mile descent through Grapevine Canyon takes you from pinyon pine country at close to 6,000 feet back down to the hot desert floor. In the narrows of the canyon, look for mule deer near the springs.

About 23 miles from the Grapevine turnoff and well out onto the valley floor you reach the salt works. This vast field of salt, in unusually high-purity deposits, was worked from around the turn of the century until the 1930s. Then, as now, the problem was access, and the miners' solution was one of the engineering wonders of the day. The large wooden towers you see here are the remains of the Saline Valley aerial salt tram, built between 1911 and 1913. Powered by huge electric motors, it carried salt from the 1,100-foot-elevation valley floor up Daisy Canyon to the Inyo Crest (8,500 feet), then down to Swansea (3,600 feet) on the east shore of Owens Lake, a total of 13.5 miles.

Shortly beyond the salt works the road passes the Saline Valley salt marsh. Lush mesquite thickets provide cover for a diversity of wildlife, including ringtail

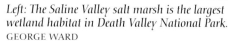

Left: The Saline Valley salt marsh is the largest wetland habitat in Death Valley National Park. GEORGE WARD
Below: Migrant species, such as the long-billed dowitcher (shown here), stop over at Saline Valley salt marsh. B. "MOOSE" PETERSON

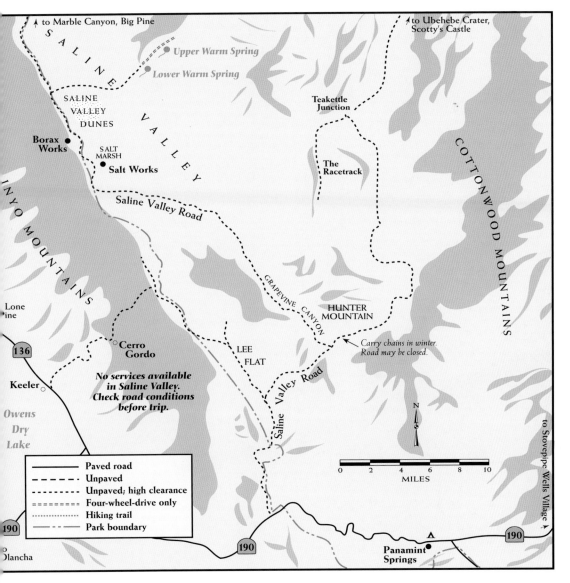

to Marble Canyon, Big Pine

to Ubehebe Crater, Scotty's Castle

Upper Warm Spring

Lower Warm Spring

S A L I N E   V A L L E Y

SALINE VALLEY DUNES

Teakettle Junction

I N Y O   M O U N T A I N S

Borax Works

SALT MARSH

Salt Works

The Racetrack

C O T T O N W O O D   M O U N T A I N S

Saline Valley Road

GRAPEVINE CANYON

HUNTER MOUNTAIN

Lone Pine

○ **Cerro Gordo**

LEE FLAT

Saline Valley Road

Carry chains in winter. Road may be closed.

136

Keeler ○

No services available in Saline Valley. Check road conditions before trip.

Owens Dry Lake

N

190

Olancha

	Paved road
	Unpaved
	Unpaved; high clearance
	Four-wheel-drive only
	Hiking trail
	Park boundary

0 2 4 6 8 10

MILES

190

190

Panamint Springs

to Stovepipe Wells Village

cats, kit foxes, red–spotted toads, biting flies, and, at last count, 124 species of visiting and resident birds.

Gold mining became serious business along the east face of the Inyo Mountains in the 1870s. The remains of mining operations are still visible clinging to the mountain face. Everything, including the parts for massive stamp mills, was hauled in by pack mules on hand–built trails.

The road continues north, past the ruins of the Conn and Trudo Borax Works that date to the 1870s. Determined hot springs aficionados can take a side trip to Upper and Lower Warm Springs for a soak in these middle–of–nowhere springs. The atmosphere here is peaceful; the pools are surrounded by palm trees and connected by rock–lined paths. The most reliable access route is a 7.5–mile washboard road that turns east off Saline Valley Road just north of the sand dunes.

Near the north end of Saline Valley, in Marble Canyon, Saline Valley Road passes several excellent examples of small–scale gold placer–mining operations. These weathered head–frames and rusting grizzlies and trommels illustrate the crude but effective techniques of river–bottom mining. From here you can continue on out of the Park to Big Pine (about 20 miles) or return the way you came.

DIRECTORY OF SERVICES

	FURNACE CREEK	STOVEPIPE WELLS	PANAMINT SPRINGS RES.	SCOTTY'S CASTLE	EMIGRANT (Campground)	MAHOGANY (Campground)	MESQUITE (Campground)	THORNDIKE (Campground)	WILDROSE (Campground)
Accommodations	WS	WS	WS						
Airport	WS	WS							
Auto Repair	WS								
Books	WS	WS	WS	WS					
Campgrounds	WS (3)	W	WS		S	S*	WS	S*	WS+
Diesel	WS								
Gasoline	WS	WS	WS	WS					
General Store	WS	WS							
Gift Shop	WS	WS	WS	WS					
Golf Course	WS								
Groceries	WS	WS	WS						
Horseback Rides	WS								
Ice	WS	WS		WS					
Laundromat	WS								
Post Office	WS								
Ranger Station	WS	WS		WS					
Restaurant	WS	WS	WS						
Showers	WS	WS	WS						
Snack Bar	WS	WS	WS	WS					
Telephone	WS	WS	WS**	WS	WS				
Worship Services	WS	W							

In case of emergency: Contact any Park Ranger or call 911 or (760) 786–2330, 24 hours a day

Park Headquarters: (760) 786-3200

W = Winter
S = Summer

* no water year–round
+ no water in winter
**emergency phone only

INDEX

The Death Valley Natural
History Association is a
non–profit educational
organization dedicated to
the preservation and
interpretation of Death
Valley National Park.
Proceeds from DVNHA
sales are used to aid
National Park Service
programs. For more infor–
mation, please contact:

Death Valley NHA
P.O. Box 188
Death Valley,
CA 92328
(760) 786–2146

Wildflowers bloom on an alluvial fan near Artist Drive.
WILLIAM M. SMITHEY, JR.